D1726561

THE MAP:
OFF WITH THE OLD...
ON WITH THE NEW

THE MAP:
OFF WITH THE OLD...
ON WITH THE NEW

DON BETTS

XULON PRESS

Xulon Press
2301 Lucien Way #415
Maitland, FL 32751
407.339.4217
www.xulonpress.com

Unless otherwise indicated, Scripture quotations taken from the Holman Christian Standard Bible (HCSB). Copyright © 1999, 2000, 2002, 2003, 2009 by Holman Bible Publishers, Nashville Tennessee. All rights reserved.

Printed in the United States of America

Paperback ISBN-13: 978-1-6628-0145-7
Hard Cover ISBN-13: 978-1-6628-0146-4
Ebook ISBN-13: 978-1-6628-0147-1

When I was a child many times in church I remember my father would ask my mother to go to the piano and accompany him on a song. He would lead the congregation in singing this chorus. I had never heard this song from anyone else...just Dad.

The best thing in my life I ever did do,
Yes, the best thing in my life I ever did do;
Oh, the best thing in my life I ever did do
Was to take off the old robe and put on the new.

The old robe was dirty all tattered and torn,
But the new robe was spotless, had never been worn;
And the best thing in my life I ever did do
Was to take off the old robe and put on the new.

Jack Pearson

I have known Pastor Don Betts for several years. This book captures perfectly, his many experiences of evangelism and Don's love for God and people. I have never been out of the country with Don's team, but I have served with a mission he has directed in America, and I know firsthand his deep love of sharing the Gospel and reaching the souls of people with it. Don truly lives out the MAP of Colossians Chapter 3. I've seen it, witnessed it in his life, and even my own family has been blessed by it.

While reading this, I am reminded of what it means to have been set free of sin, so that I can LIVE free! All for the Glory of God!

—-Holly Verburg

"From spreading the words of Jesus Christ behind the crumbling Iron Curtain to the Middle East and Africa, and to the inner cities of Ohio in outreach and service to at-risk young people, evangelist and pastor Don Betts has led a life that only few can claim: that of somebody who has set his mind on what is above. Don has an authentic, deep, and abiding faith in the will and provision of the Lord and our Savior and an unswerving desire and devotion to living out the calling of the Great Commission to share the Gospel. I have had the great privilege over years of listening to him share his captivating stories of international and local evangelism mission work, sharing a message of hope and the mutual faith between Lord and servant that we can have with our Heavenly Father and His Son. You as a reader may now enjoy the benefit of being able to read Don's stories and carry away from this book some of the insights that I gained along the way from Don."

—-Marshall Haker

Obeying the indisputable call of God, Pastor Don Betts takes us on his journey of faith woven through the book of Colossians, inspiring a call to action in our own pursuit of Christ.

—-Danica Allen–a life encouraged by the journey of Don Betts

Don Betts is a man of God, faithful preacher of the Gospel, church planter, and devoted family man. Both of our children came to the Lord under Don's preaching, and he and his wife, Linda, are close personal friends and great encouragers. His ministry of evangelism has impacted thousands of lives, both here in the states and in many other countries around the world. God used him greatly in Ukraine, where he led citywide crusades in multiple locations around the country. I consider it a blessing to call him my friend and fellow servant of the Lord Jesus Christ.

—-Peter Hamilton, Pastor of First Baptist Church, Marysville, Ohio

ACKNOWLEDGMENTS

Each crusade listed in this book was a great success because of leaders who were gifted by God to plan, organize and advertise in each city. I want to especially thank Illya Shmilikovskyy who gave his life to organize each European Crusade to reach people with the Gospel of Jesus Christ. Illya assembled a team that was used by God to bring thousands of people to God.

Thank you, Illya.

I also want to thank Chaouki Boulos for organizing and promoting evangelistic celebrations in Lebanon, Jordan and Egypt. Your work helped reach thousands with the Gospel of Jesus Christ which touched lives throughout the Middle East countries.

Thank you, Chaouki.

There is one person who has served God with all her strength to help make all these crusades and celebrations a success. I want to thank my wife, Linda, for the work and patience she has given through all the years. She has served as Wife, Mother,

CEO, Secretary, Financial Accountant and whatever it took for this work to be successful. Her value is greater than all. Thank you, Linda. I love you more than anything!

TABLE OF CONTENTS

PREFACE

Several people have asked me to write about the experiences in my life from our international evangelistic ministry. God has taken us to places that I had never dreamed to go. Most of our ministry was localized in the countries of Ukraine and Russia. I was met at the airport in Kyiv, Ukraine, one day and my driver told me that he was taking me on an eight-hour ride to meet someone special. I asked him why, but all he said was that he wanted to meet me. When we arrived I was escorted into a house where I saw a man sitting with a radiant smile. His name was Illya Shmilikhovskyy. He had been trained by the Billy Graham Association to be a Crusade Director for mass evangelism events. After meeting and talking a while, he told me that he had been following our ministry in Ukraine and wanted to know if he could set up an evangelistic crusade in a capital city where I would be invited to preach. I agreed and a few months later I returned to preach the crusade messages in Ternopil, Ukraine. There were huge crowds each evening and many people who made decisions to follow Christ.

Following the crusade, Illya asked if he could do one more evangelistic crusade preparation for me to preach. I agreed and later returned to L'viv, Ukraine, where again the crowds were great and the number of people receiving Christ was great.

God had gifted Illya to do this work. I saw God use him to prepare huge events to bring thousands of people to hear the Gospel of Jesus Christ.

Following this crusade, Illya asked if he could come on the staff of the Don Betts Evangelistic Association and prepare crusades fulltime. Our board of directors agreed and we began leading evangelistic events in Ukraine, Russia, and Poland. Later God opened the opportunity for evangelistic events in Lebanon, Egypt, Syria, Jordan, and Kenya.

I am grateful to God for allowing me to work with Illya and our team for several years. God gave to us a great team.

In this book, I have shared many of the stories that came from those crusade experiences. From multiple death threats to the thousands of people crowding into venues to hear the Gospel of Jesus Christ. From the many people who came to Christ, new churches were planted and continue to this day.

Also, contained in this book is an exposition of my favorite chapter in all of God's Word...Colossians chapter three. It is unique in that God gives practical teaching for you to digest. Leave the clothes of the old person in the grave and put on the new clothes that God has provided for you. This chapter is a map of your journey in life. It is a practical step-by-step teaching of what to unpack in your life and what to pack. The unpacking requires getting rid of some things. The writer says to *"put to death"* those things or *"Mortify"* some things.

It's practical and easily understood. I do my best to make it more practical and cause you to have a strong desire to come out of the graveyard of the old person and live in the freedom of the new person in Jesus Christ! Take this journey with me and get ready to pack the right stuff for the journey.

Colossians three is God's Roadmap for your life.

Like any map or GPS, you must follow the directions. Colossians three Maps it out. Let's call it

THE MAP!
WHAT TO UNPACK AND PACK FOR
THE JOURNEY

CHAPTER ONE...
THE JOURNEY BEGINS

In 1990 I saw my life take a drastic change in my work in ministry. From being a pastor...God put on my heart to leave the ministry of pastoring to do the work of evangelism. That call began in my life at the age of sixteen years old. It was 1990 and the world was making dramatic changes.

Eastern Europe was a focus of that change. I began praying for God to take me to places where others were NOT going...to go to places where the work of the Gospel was new and the work of evangelism had NOT taken place. That year I was invited by an evangelist friend of mine to go to the former Soviet Union and witness the changes God was bringing to that part of the world. We traveled through Hungary into the Soviet Republics of Ukraine and Russia. We journeyed through these countries for three weeks. I had a great time preaching, sharing the Gospel on the streets, and taking in the culture of that part of the world. It was my first journey out of America except for a couple of trips into Canada. This was an eye-opening experience for me. Each new day brought new adventures as I had never experienced before.

But, I had seen more flies swimming in tea and coffee than I had ever seen in my life. On one occasion one of my friends ran out of the restaurant where we were eating to hurl. When he returned he asked me to look at his plate. We were all given "Golubtsy" to eat (known here as cabbage rolls) and as he cut through his cabbage roll a small white worm crawled out onto his plate.

I told him it was good that it was not a HALF of a worm!

I had seen more fear of government authorities than I had ever seen. I witnessed the dictatorial mandates of politicians and denominational leaders who were socialists and communists and had caused fear in the people. I saw concrete structures built many stories high for homes (most with NO elevators) in which **most** of the people in these countries lived...etc.

One of the ministers on our team asked me as we were on a bus leaving Russia if I planned to return. Considering the lack of uncleanliness, I had witnessed including losing fifteen pounds, I immediately replied, *"NO!"* He responded by saying, *"You should. God has given to you a gift to reach these people for Him."*

His words ping-ponged in my head and heart for the next several months. I told God that I didn't have the money. I mentioned to Him how much different the culture was from what I was accustomed to.

I also jogged God's memory that I had no other contacts for an invitation to return. Without an invitation, I could not apply for a Visa.

So, what did God do during those next few months?

First, He intensified my love for the people of that part of the world each time I shared my story concerning the trip. And, I shared my story often!

Second, soon after I returned home I received a letter from one of the state presidents in Ukraine who attended a church where I spoke and he gave to me an official invitation to lead evangelistic crusades in his state.

Third, a cardiologist who I had met earlier in a church in Pennsylvania sent me a letter. He had heard me preach in a church that he had attended and the letter included a $2,000-dollar gift for continued work oversees...the amount needed to go.

Fourth and finally, an evangelist friend of mine called me and asked me to go with him to Hungary and Romania.

Do you see the problem here? Every excuse that I had given for NOT returning had been taken from me. ALL OF THEM!

So, I went back with my friend and preached in Hungary and Romania. We took Bibles and commentaries translated into their native languages.

Then, in August of 1991, I was in Ukraine the day they declared their independence from the Soviet Union. In reality, they were separating from Russia.

So, God began taking me places where others had not gone with the Gospel. Then God gave me a confirmation of His intentions in 1993. I was leading a team for evangelism and we were in Moscow, Russia.

My oldest son was with me and we celebrated his sixteenth birthday in Moscow. Our main interpreter, Tonya, met us for breakfast one morning. She came over to me excited about something. I asked her why all the excitement. She said, *"Before I went to bed last night God revealed something to me. He gave to me a passage of scripture and told me it was for Don Betts. I opened the scripture and read it."* She opened her Russian Bible and I opened my English Bible and we read it together. It says, *"Moses My servant is dead. Now you and all the people prepare to cross over Jordan to the land I am giving the Israelites. I have given you every place where the sole of your foot treads, just as I promised Moses...No one will be able to stand against you as long as you live.*
I will be with you, just as I was with Moses. I will not leave you or forsake you." Joshua 1:2-5
God had answered my prayers long before I took the journey into evangelism.

The stories in this book interrupt the commentary on Colossians numerous times. Stories of events in Russia, Ukraine, Poland, Hungary, Romania, Israel, Lebanon, Jordan, Egypt, Kenya, and America. What God has done in these countries is nothing short of miraculous.

Get ready. What you are about to read is not only about real-life people and events that God has directed, but, it tells the story of a chapter in the Bible that quickly became my favorite passage and I know will speak to you in a life-changing way.

So, the journey begins...Get packed and follow **THE MAP!**

CHAPTER TWO...
LAZARUS, WHERE ARE YOU?

COLOSSIANS 3...

Several years ago I had the privilege of hearing a gentleman lead the Bible Study sessions in a conference for ministers. His study throughout the conference was on the letter of Colossians. His teaching of this book prompted me to go deeper and study it much more. But, I remember he began the study of chapter three with a story. I have told this story hundreds of times since then (maybe with some different twists and turns, yet, the same context.)

Let's take a little trip in our minds right now. You may feel like you need a trip.
Imagine we are standing in a valley in the village of Bethany, just outside Jerusalem. There is a huge crowd gathered there on this rather warm morning.
We notice the crowd is especially gathered around a hole in the side of a hill...covered by a large rock. It's a tomb. Behind

that rock, several people have been buried. There was one person buried there that had the crowd concerned.

His name is Lazarus, someone everyone knew in that community and everyone loved. Lazarus was a friend to many people, but, four days ago he died. He just got sick and eventually died. His two sisters, Mary and Martha, were devastated by his death as were many of his friends who had gathered that day.

The reason for the crowd is interesting.

Lazarus and his family were good friends with a man claiming to be the Messiah...Jesus Christ. The word had gotten around that Jesus was coming to Bethany that day to raise Lazarus from the dead.

But...there were many skeptics in the crowd. You see, many of them believed a tale that said up to three days after a person dies their spirit remains with the body, and resurrection is a possibility.

BUT, Jesus had waited too long. Lazarus' body had been in the tomb...dead...for four days. So, to all, it was futile to even assume that Lazarus would ever resurrect from the dead.

Imagine standing there in the crowd of people that day.

The morning turns to noon and Jesus has not appeared. Let's imagine we can understand what people are saying. Doubters began speaking freely.

Someone says, *"I bet He doesn't show up. He's simply given false hope to all of us."*

Someone else says, *"Who does He think He is? I know His parents. This Jesus is just a man like us and cannot resurrect anyone. He's only human. He bleeds like all of us. There's nothing special about Him."*

As the day wears on the doubters grow in number.
Finally, someone from the top of one of the hills cups his hands around his mouth and begins to yell, *"HE'S COMING... HE'S COMING!"*
Everyone in the valley looks toward the one crying out to see if it's true.
Sure enough, a crowd of people begins walking over the hill and down into the valley. Someone says, *"It's Him! I've seen Him before and that's him!"*

We are standing there in disbelief. It's really Jesus. He has really come.
We notice Martha and Mary, Lazarus' sisters, walk up to say something to Jesus. Martha said something like this. *"Lord, if You had been here my brother would not have died..."* Jesus said, *"Your brother will rise!"* He reminded her that He was the *"resurrection and the life."*

So He goes to the opening of the tomb and asked for the stone to be rolled away. Martha reminded Jesus that his body has been in the tomb for four days and his body is already beginning to stink!

Then Jesus looks up to heaven and begins to pray.
All of us are listening to what He is praying. He says something like this. *"Father, I want to thank You that You always hear Me and that You already have this thing worked out. But, so that*

THESE PEOPLE who are listening will know that you are God..."
Then He looks into the hole in the side of the hill and shouted,
"LAZARUS, COME OUT!"

A little boy was going home with his family from church one
Sunday when his mother asked him what he studied in Sunday
School. He said, *"We learned about Lazarus when he died and
Jesus came to raise him from the dead. Mom...did you know
that when Jesus said 'LAZARUS, COME FORTH' that if He just
said 'COME FORTH' that His voice was so powerful that every
dead person on earth would have come alive!!!"*

Now, back to Bethany, our trip makes a dramatic change. You
and I are standing there with the others looking into that hole
when suddenly we see a body...wrapped in cloths...coming out
of that tomb!

People are astonished. Some are scared. Jesus tells the
people to unwrap him and let him loose. They do as He says.
IT'S LAZARUS!

There is more joy in the valley that day than anyone has
ever seen!

Everyone wants to talk to Lazarus. Everyone wants to talk to
Jesus! The crowd becomes a "holy mob!"

Someone says, *"I'm from the Jerusalem Gazette"* and I have a
couple of questions, Lazarus.

*"Tell me, what was it like being dead for four days? Would you
say that this is the most exciting day of your life?"*

(Asking stupid questions by the media has never changed!)

When the afternoon was turning into early evening, the crowd begins to disperse back to their homes. Now, Martha, Lazarus' older sister, asked Jesus if He would like to come to their house for supper. They live in Bethany and they are close so Jesus says, *"Sure...that'd be great."*

Again, this is our trip and we are still with them.
They begin their journey to their house when Martha decides to say something to Lazarus, her brother.
"Lazarus," she says. There is no response.
"Lazarus, where are you?"
Frustrated, she turns to the younger sister, Mary, and asked, *"Mary, where is your brother?"*
"I don't know" was her reply. *"I thought he was with us."*
Martha tells Mary, the younger sister,
"You go and find your brother and tell him he better not be late for supper. Jesus is our guest and he better get home quickly!"
(By the way, you know how ladies are when you're late for supper. Not GOOD!)
So, Mary retraced her steps back to the valley.
Now, it's getting dark outside and she's not sure how she feels about going back to where the dead are buried.
She gets to the top of the hill and calls out in the valley, *"Lazarus!"* There is no answer. A little louder she calls out, *"Lazarus, where are you!!"* She takes a few steps closer to the valley where it is getting dark and cries out, *"Lazarus, where are you. Jesus is coming to our house for supper...Lazarus, Martha told me to find you and tell you NOT TO BE LATE... Lazarus, Martha is MAD!!!"*

Again, there was no answer. So Mary ventures down to where Lazarus lay dead for the past four days. The rock was still moved from the opening so she got close and shouted in the tomb.

"Lazarus, are you in there?"

"Yeah, Mary, come on in" Lazarus replied.

Mary was shocked. She saw her brother, Lazarus sitting in the place where he had laid for four days...putting the old grave clothes back on.

"Lazarus, what are you doing?" Mary said. *"Jesus is coming to our house for supper...Martha is very angry with you and said for you NOT to be late...Lazarus, what in the world are you doing?"*

Lazarus told Mary to settle down and not get too excited.

"Mary, I've been in this place for four days.

After four days these clothes are just beginning to fit good and... you get used to the smell once you're in here for a while. Go back home and tell Martha that I have decided to make this place...the grave...my new home!"

NOW, I ask you. Is that what took place?

I was in a church in the country of Ukraine with my evangelism team when I told that story. There were around 1500 people present. There were about fifteen people on our team and we ate lunch together following the Sunday morning worship. I noticed they were all involved in a conversation so I asked what it was all about.

They began to tell me that when I added to the story about Jesus going home with them for supper and Lazarus deciding to live in the grave...the people knew the story, as I told it, was NOT in the Bible.

One of the guys said their faces were filled with anger and he thought they were ready to throw me out!

But, when I told them that I had exaggerated the story...then the congregation took a deep breath of relief and relaxed.

Look...Colossians chapter three...my favorite chapter of the entire Bible...begins by saying,

CHAPTER THREE...
THE MAP AND PRAYER

"If or (since) you have been raised with Christ, seek what is above, where Christ is seated at the right hand of God."

So, the question is, have you been raised with Jesus Christ? Do you have a personal relationship with Him?

You will have little or no desire to "put to death" earthly gain if you have never begun a relationship with Jesus Christ. It simply will not make sense to you.

Why trade what's in your hand...in your possession...for something that you cannot see? It's a crazy deal.

But, that's what a relationship with God is all about. It means putting your Faith...Trust...in God, whom you cannot see, and let Him take care of your earthly stuff...regardless of how much you have accumulated.

So, since you have a relationship with Jesus Christ you now have been raised with Him.

Some have stated that the theme of the entire letter of Colossians is found in chapter one and verse eighteen. It reads:

"He (Jesus) is the head of the body,
the church
He is the beginning,
the firstborn from the dead,
So that He might come to have
FIRST PLACE IN EVERYTHING!"

This verse gives you a good perspective on what it means to be in Christ. While in Christ you give Him everything. You "seek" for things that are related to Christ.

Look at the first four verses:
"So if you have been raised with Messiah (Jesus Christ), seek what is above, where the Messiah (Christ) is, seated at the right hand of God.
Set your minds on what is above, not on what is on the earth.
For you have died, and your life is hidden with the Messiah in God.
When the Messiah, who is your life, is revealed, then you also will be revealed with Him in glory."
3:1-4

I offer to you the opinion that when you give your life to Jesus Christ you will find it **natural** to want to live your life for Him. You will find it less conflicting to "seek" Him.
Why?
When your life is in Christ you are conflicted when you seek earthly stuff. Come on…you know I'm right about this.

If "money" becomes more important to you than reading God's Word or praying and having personal time with God or serving Him in your church...You become conflicted about your priorities.

You've been there. Admit it! There have been times in your life when you have leaned or **jumped** into the earthly stuff and ignored seeking God.
RIGHT?
Maybe you're there now. Maybe there is conflict in your life... in your heart...in your mind...because you are not seeking Messiah as much as you are seeking the earthly stuff.

The remedy? *'Seek what is above!"* How do you do that?

First, get alone with God! Seriously alone!
Isaiah 26:20 says,
"Go, my people, enter your rooms and close your doors behind you."

I am amazed at how Jesus could **not** have given clearer instructions on how to spend time with God. I'll try to make it easier to understand by giving you a step-by-step map in finding the place and taking the time to spend time **alone** with God. AND...God will show up to your personal meeting. Jesus said He would. Here it is:

Matthew 6:6 says,
"But when you Pray, go into your private room, SHUT YOUR DOOR, and Pray to your Father who is in secret.

And your Father who sees in secret will reward you."
Seeking what is above means seeking God...Personally...Alone...
In private! You do not and cannot have worldly distractions
around you while you are seeking God.
"Shut the Door."

THAT, my friend, is how you *"Seek what is above..."* and
*"Set your minds on what is above and NOT on what is on
the earth!"*

(A step-by-step detail of THE PRAYER MAP is given in chapter
thirteen.)

CHAPTER FOUR...
THE MAP AND THE BIBLE

A nother way to **"seek what is above"** is to love His Word... the Bible...and read and learn from it so you can apply its principles to your life, daily.

I never realized how much people loved God's Word until my experience with a gentleman in the former Soviet Union.

I had ridden a bus from Austria to Uzhgorod, Ukraine. At that time, it was still considered the Soviet Union. I knew a few Russian words like...gift, thank you, your welcome, hello, God, Jesus Christ, God loves you, toilet...and a few more. So, I took several salvation pamphlets and a Russian Bible and my Bible and began walking down the street alone. When I passed someone I would hold out a pamphlet and say the Russian word for "Gift" ...Padarik. They would answer with a "Thank you" ...Spaseba. I would say "Your Welcome" ...Diakuyu and then walk on to the next person. After a few minutes, three young ladies...sixteen and seventeen years old...each took a pamphlet. They giggled and I walked on. Then I heard one of them say in English..." Thank you." Suddenly I thought, "*I know*

that language!" I turned and said, *"Do you speak English?"*
One of the girls...named Natalie...said, *"Yes, a little bit."*
We began a conversation...in English. Her friends did not speak
English. Their names were Zhanet and Vika. They wanted to
know why I was in their city. I told them that we had brought
75,000 Bibles translated into Russian to give to local churches
and believers. Also, we had come to share with them what the
pamphlet explained...How to know that God loves you and
how to begin a new life in Him.
My Russian Bible had been marked to go from one passage
to another to share the Gospel. I shared with Natalie and she
translated the Gospel to her friends. It was really awesome!!!
When I asked if they would like to receive Jesus Christ into
their lives...each girl said *"Yes."* So, I led Natalie in prayer and
she led her two friends!
They all prayed to receive Jesus into their lives.

Then, they asked me if they could take me to the center of the
city to show me their town. I said *"Yes"* and we began walking.
After a few minutes, we were in the city center and there were
thousands of people milling around for various reasons. There
were vendors on the streets selling their wares and plenty of
people buying them. I noticed one elderly lady selling flowers...
long-stemmed roses.
I walked up to her and offered to her a pamphlet and said,
"Padarik" ...Gift. She gave me the sign to wait for a moment
and I noticed she took one of her roses and reached out to
me and said, *"Padarik."*

I took the rose and said, *"Spaseba"* ...Thank you. When I turned around I noticed there were hundreds of people gathered around me watching our exchange.

I asked Natalie if she would translate for me as I share the message that I had shared with her and her two friends earlier. She agreed...so we shared the Gospel.

Then, an elderly man, he looked to be in his eighties, standing near me in the crowd, shouted out something. I asked Natalie what he had said. She said, *"He wants your Bible."* He wanted my English Bible. I told her to tell him that I could not give Him my Bible. So, he asked if he could **see** my Bible. I opened my Bible and put it out for him to see. I will never forget how he approached my Bible. He cleaned his hands as meticulously as he could and placed one hand on one page of my Bible and the other hand on the opposite page. He leaned forward and kissed the Bible and then took my hand and kissed it. Then he said something and walked away and I never saw him again. I asked Natalie what he had said and she translated, *"He said 'thank you' and then he said 'that's the first time in my life that I have ever seen a Bible!'"*

Eighty years old and had **never** seen a Bible.

And, the first time he saw the Bible he treated it as if it were the most precious thing he had ever seen. He had never seen the Bible, yet, he loved the Bible...God's Word!!!

I came away from that experience realizing how much more reverence I needed to give to God's Word. I realized how important God's Word was intended to be in my life and that I was to share it with others.

Another way we *"Seek what is above and Set our minds on what is above and not on earth..."* is to read, study, and share God's Holy Word...the Bible!

If the people who know you and are a part of your life could be asked what they think is the most important thing to you... in your life...what would they say?
Would they say that they notice how much you love Jesus Christ?
Would they say that they notice much you love the Word of God?

When you *"Seek"* God first and He is *"First Place"* in your life... it shows. You don't hide it. You live it. You love it. You long for it.

Why do you live like this? Because, in a sense, it's not YOU living, but, it's Messiah.
You have died to your old self and are letting God live through you.
You literally, physically, and spiritually are hidden in Him. You see, you don't want the world to see **you**...**you** want them to see **JESUS!**

And the really cool thing about this is when your time on earth is finished and Christ returns to earth to wrap all this stuff up... YOU'LL BE WITH HIM!

Wait a second...Look at that again more intently.
"When Christ, who IS YOUR LIFE, is revealed, then YOU also will be revealed with Him in glory!" v. 4.

Yes, it means what it says and says what it means.

Our Messiah will someday be revealed again. And when He appears...you will be revealed with him. Paul told the Romans that one day the sons of God will be revealed. *"For the creation eagerly awaits with anticipation for God's sons to be revealed."* **Romans 8:19.**

This would give to us the reason for the subject matter that follows in the remainder of Colossians chapter 3. He tells us what to get rid of in our lives...what to unpack...and then he tells us what to use for its' replacement...what to pack.

Get rid of the sin in your life. Sexual sin, lust, evil desires, greed... just to name a few...are to be confessed and put into the grave-yard of sin. Unpacked from your life's journey.

It is a call for people to get cleaned up before the great feast comes. When you appear with Messiah at His next coming... His desire is for you to be presented clean and spotless.

To be honest, it means that TODAY is a good day to begin your clean walk in the Lord. This is a good time for you to begin your preparation to meet Jesus and let Him present you "CLEAN."

Okay...the process begins in verse 5.

CHAPTER FIVE...
LOVE YOUR UNDERTAKER

D o you know what *"Mortify"* means? In Colossians 3:5 some Bible versions say to *"Mortify"* whatever is worldly in your bodies. Other versions give the meaning of the word by saying, *"Put to death"* the worldly stuff that is in your bodies. *"Put to death!"* **Unpack it.**

You do know what a Mortician is...don't you?
He is the Undertaker. The guy that takes care of you when you die.
I was told that you need to be best friends with your undertaker because he is always the last person to let you down!!! (Ha Ha...Knee Slapper...)

Here is what the Bible says and why it says it:
Colossians 3:5-7:
"Therefore, put to death whatever in you is worldly: sexual immorality, impurity, lust, evil desire, and greed, which is idolatry.
Because of these, God's wrath comes on the disobedient, and you once walked in these things when you were living in them.

So, if one or more of these is present in your life...it is in your best interest to rid yourself of them. Unpack it. Mortify it. Kill it.

The result of worldly ways in your life is that God's wrath is lingering over the sin that is in your life. He is waiting for you to become obedient to Him rather than disobedient to Him and keep hanging on to them.

You see, living with worldliness in your life is disobedience to God. It's the way you lived when you were **not** a Christ-follower. If worldliness remains in your life...what is your life saying to the world? It says, *"I'm more interested in ME than I am God."* It says, *"I want what looks good...feels good...sounds good and I am NOT interested in living my life for God!"*

People see you as living for yourself and **not** for God.

You are a godless, impure, selfish, self-centered, spiritually bankrupt human being. Are you dealing with sexual immorality?

Gallup reported that in America sexual impurity is increasing. For example:

Divorce—73%

Sex between an unmarried man and woman—69%

Having a baby outside of marriage—62%

Sex between teenagers—36%

Pornography—36%

Polygamy—17%

Extramarital affairs—9%

Then, there is the broader immorality which includes impurity...anyone that is bound sexually to relationships outside of marriage and beyond. The same is true concerning evil desire and lust. Some Bibles call this *"Evil Concupiscence."* It is evil in the mind...in the conscience. You know what I mean. For example, pornography!

America leads the world in the making of and use of porn. Evil minds!!!
To look at porn is to FEED the worldly sin of sexual impurity.
It is the beginning of unraveling your marriage.
It is the beginning of destroying your children.
It is the beginning of destroying your relationship with a loving, all-powerful God who loves you extremely.
To participate in such behavior will bring on the wrath of God in your life.
"Because of these, God's wrath comes on the disobedient!" v. 6.

Rid yourself of these things. How?
Go into your prayer closet and ask God what He wants you to do. Take your pen and paper and listen to God.

USE THE PRAYER MAP! (Chapter 13)
Confess them and claim God's forgiveness...1 John 1:9...and leave your Prayer Closet forgiven...Changed.
The time and money you have used for your worldliness can **now** be used for Godliness!

Second, make a new plan for your future. Begin with priorities. Remember, the theme of the letter of Colossians is:

"He (Jesus) is the Head of the body, the church; He is the beginning, the firstborn from the dead, so that He might come to have FIRST PLACE IN EVERYTHING!" Col. 1:18.

There is a simple way to know if you have Jesus as first place in your life. Ask your family. Ask your friends. Ask the people who see you often. They see and know where your priorities lie. If God is number one...they will affirm it. On the other hand, if something else is number one in your life (like maybe YOU) they will affirm that as well.

It's simple for you to know. Are you doing the things that cause spiritual growth in your life? Are you having Personal and Family Prayer times? Are you having Bible reading AND Bible study? Are you serving God in various capacities in your life? Oh, yes...you know what is your priority.

I remember one night in the Rivne region of Ukraine our team was leading an evangelistic crusade in a District Center city. We were in a Philharmonic Hall. The Hall was overflowing with about 2,000 people present. While I was sharing the message of the Gospel of Jesus Christ there was a man who was knocking on the door at the rear entrance of the hall.

The vice president (VP) of one of the main denominations opened the door. The man was curious as to what was going on in his city. He saw me preaching and asked who I was. He told him and then said that I was from America.

The man pointed his finger toward me and said, "My god has told me to come here tonight and kill that man!"

The VP summoned another man to assist him in getting the man out the door.

We continued our crusade without knowing what was happening behind us. I concluded the message and the invitation. Many people gathered at the front of the stage to pray with counselors and receive Jesus into their lives.

During the counseling, the VP came in from the rear of the stage and shouted to me that a man outside the rear exit wants to meet me. I replied, *"Okay"* and proceeded to get on the stage and walk toward the rear door.

While I was walking across the stage to the door the VP said, *"He has come here to kill you! He is filled with a demon."* That's a good piece of information to know.

So, immediately I began to open my Bible to the story where Jesus prayed the demons out of the man who was living in the cemetery. Then, one of the guys from America who went with me asked if I wanted him to go also. At first, I replied *"No"* and then just before opening the door I looked up at Terry…a former football player in his University, built like a football player, and I said, *"Yes, Terry, come with me."*

When we got outside I noticed this man standing in front of me. He grabbed my arms and said, *"I have come to kill you!"* Later I discovered that he was known around the city as *"Freddie, the killer."*

I grabbed him by the head and put him in a headlock. I told him that *"The God who is in me is greater than the god that is in you and you are NOT going to kill me."* Then he fell to his knees and began barking like a dog. He kept yelling *"Sobaka, Sobaka!"* (That's the Russian word for "Dog.") Then he bit the leg of the VP.

Finally, he told me that when his grandmother was on her death bed, she told him that an evil spirit would enter him and the only way he would be delivered would be by an American believer. We talked and prayed for several minutes and then Freddie began to cry.

I asked him what happened? He said, *"For the first time in years...since my grandmother died...I felt that the evil spirit was gone!"* It had left him!

Freddie stood up and gently took my arm, looked into my eyes, and said, *"Will you be my friend? I have no friends."* I agreed to be his friend.

Some of our people had brought cameras with them and Freddie asked if he could have a picture of us. When we walked through the door of the Hall, many people were on their knees praying.

I heard gasps from several people who shouted, *"He's a killer!"* The VP assured them that Freddie had given his life to Jesus Christ and was no longer wanting to kill anyone.

Satan, Freddie's god, had told him that an American was in his city and that his job was to *"put him to death!"*

You see, the Devil is not happy with God's children. He is not pleased when we surrender our lives to Christ and put to death the immoral pleasures of this world.

CHAPTER SIX...
WHAT ANGER?

Mortify the worldliness in your life. "Put it to Death!"

Furthermore, there's more stuff we need to unpack in our lives.

"But now you are also to put away all the following: anger, wrath, malice, slander, and filthy language from your mouth." V.8

I t is at this point that most Christ-followers agree with every-thing that has been said. They will agree that sexual immo-rality is bad. Lust is bad. Sinful thoughts are bad. Greed is bad. BUT, when we talk about the next sin...Anger...the agreements cease. Why?
Because believers are just as guilty as anyone when it comes to getting angry. Anger is just the beginning. Let's go...

We begin with the one we recognize the most...ANGER!
Do you have a problem with ANGER?
Seriously, are you the kind of person who gets ANGRY easily?
Are you the grouch in your home?

I admit that when I was younger I had some anger issues. Really. I think it began when my family moved from Kansas City, Missouri, to Cleveland, Ohio. I was ten years old when we moved. We moved in the summer and I began attending a new school in September. It seemed to me that the Civil War was still fresh in my classmates' minds. They knew I had moved from Missouri...which they thought was the South. I also carried a bit of a southern accent which didn't help. So, I was called "Rebel" while they took on the tag as "Yankee." It was fun to pick on the new kid...the "Rebel." It was a time that I had to fight off each "Yankee" ...literally, FIGHT! Several guys thought fighting me would prove that the Yankees were better than the Rebels.

By the way, the name of my school was Ulysses Grant Elementary School. Its very name was from a Yankee General in the Civil War.

I think that's where my anger issues began.
They made me mad...often. I had to defend myself and putting on an attitude of anger seemed to help deter some of the battles.

I eventually went to a local high school.
The name of my high school was the Willoughy South High School "Rebels." By the time I attended high school the Civil War had ended with my classmates. In fact, it ended when I left Grant elementary.

But, I noticed that using my anger for my advantage was still effective. On several occasions such as in sports, music, school council...I noticed that deep inside of me the anger issue still existed. It stayed with me throughout my college days and into my years as an adult.

I remember the days when my father was young and how he also had to deal with anger. Dad was the greatest influence on how to be a child of God. He and I were closet friends when I became an adult.

But, if I were to do something rebellious or hateful as a child... he could pull his belt off quicker than Matt Dillon could draw his gun from his holster. The one thing that I never desired was to make my father angry with me.

But, I did. Several times.

This made me realize something about dealing with a contagious sin like "Anger." Angry people make you want to run from them. It's the opposite of kindness. As the son of my father, I realized the impression it made on my life.

But, the older I got I realized that my father dealt with it and God gave him victory over it. He was the greatest father a son could have. He loved God with all his heart. It made me realize that even when he was angry, he still loved God more than anything. The thing I had to do was grow up and realize his heart. Evidence proves that God continues to work in us to grow us up in Him.

Yes...even adults need to continue to grow. I can only hope that people will do the same for me.

It is something that zings inside of you. When someone makes you mad...you feel it inside. It's like electricity...it bites you. When you get angry you feel it. But, many times it is contained and you do not react.

What if someone walked up to you and criticized your new hairdo or haircut? Immediately you get that "zing" feeling and you get mad. What right do they have to criticize your new look? NONE! You're thinking, *"Mind your own business. Who cares what you think!"*

But, you, the holy person you are...the kind person you are... keeps it all inside. That's anger!
Have you ever felt it? Have you ever experienced the "Zing?" Sure you have. Many times! The number one thing you need to do when you get zinged by anger is PRAY. Ask God to forgive your anger and get it behind you.
If you don't...it will snowball into something worse.

Now, let's suppose you go home and you're speaking to someone on the phone and you "happen" to bring up the person who criticized your new look. Now, what are you doing? That's right...YOU ARE GOSSIPING! That's wrath.
You have now acted upon your anger and turned it into wrath. You couldn't leave it alone. You didn't unpack it from your life by giving it to God. The snowball is rolling and getting bigger.

The Bible says,
"All bitterness, anger and wrath, insult and slander must be removed from you, along with all wickedness. AND be kind

and compassionate to one another, forgiving one another, just as God also forgave you in Christ!" Eph. 4:31-32.

Still, if you don't deal with it and give it to God, your anger will continue to escalate. You will find new ways to react and retaliate. It will turn to malice. The snowball keeps growing. Then, you will find yourself criticizing the person more and eventually adding to the story to the point that you are being slanderous and telling lies about them.

"ANGER" ...what a mean and ugly word. It is a way for Satan to get a stronghold in your life.

Getting ANGRY is a way to give the devil an entrance into your life where he will grab hold of you and will NOT voluntarily get out of your life. In fact, he will cause you to get ANGRY more and more. There will be times when you get angry and you don't even know why.

It becomes a way of life for you.

Left unchecked and unconfessed it will grow into something that you will **not** be able to control. The Bible says, *"...Don't let the sun go down on your anger, AND don't give the Devil an opportunity!" Eph. 4:26-27.*

This means that anger opens a crack in the door of your life and the Devil steps in. He grabs whatever in your life that causes you to stumble. He will grab you where you are the most vulnerable...ANGER!

Confess it. Do **not** let the Devil have an entrance into your life. Unpack it from your life. As Barney Fife would say, *"Nip it in the bud!"*

Unconfessed anger turns into wrath; unconfessed wrath turns into malice; unconfessed malice turns into slander or blasphemy; unconfessed slander will turn into filthy language... cursing...swearing...gossip.

And, unconfessed anger will eventually turn into LIES!

On a personal side, I have never seen people become so angry as I have when someone speaks about Jesus and His Gospel of salvation.

I was preaching in a stadium one day in the country of Ukraine. We were in one of the capital cities for a citywide crusade.

The stadium was filled with people and the musicians had concluded their music and it was time for me to speak.

As I was speaking, I heard a man shouting from the stands. He was somewhere off to my right. Then I heard the shouts getting louder and I looked in that direction and saw a man with a club coming toward me. He had crossed the track and was on the field running toward the platform shouting something in Russian. I kept speaking until finally, I saw three men from the music team run to the man and lift him above their shoulders and carry him off the field and out of the stadium.

When the service was completed the interpreter told me that she was frightened of that man. He was shouting to me,

"You're not Russian and I'm going to kill you! You're not Russian and I'm going to kill you!"

He was angry with me and decided to act upon his anger.

Anger...it's a bad thing. The Devil can destroy you with ANGER.

I remember leading a crusade in Amman, Jordan. Our evangelistic team was staying in a hotel near the crusade venue.

One night at 4:00 AM I was awakened by the sound of gunfire in the hotel. The director of the crusade called me and told me that I was the only American in the hotel and that I needed to stay put. I was on the fourth floor and my room faced the front of the hotel.

Out of curiosity, I opened my curtains as little as I could to see if anything was going on outside. I noticed police cars lined up in front of the hotel and officers were on the opposite side of their cars kneeling and pointing guns toward the hotel. Two men came out of the hotel lobby and began scuffling. One man, dressed in black, had a gun in his hand. They parted ways and the man with the gun walked over to a car with the engine running...opened the back door on the passenger side and fired his gun at a person sitting in the back seat. Then he turned and began walking away from the car down the street. It seemed that the police were shouting at him to stop, but, he ignored them. The next thing I heard was gunshots and the man fell to the ground to his death.

The next morning, I went to the restaurant where the shots were fired the night before. I saw a lady who worked at the hotel and I asked her if she knew what had happened.

She told me how two men became angry at each other and began arguing. One of the men had a gun. He pulled it out of his pocket and began shooting it. One of the bullets ricocheted off the marble floor and hit another man, killing him. She told me that she was there...in a nearby hallway. She and another worker pulled the man into the hallway where he later died.

What had happened? ANGER! Two guys arguing. Two guys fighting. Two men letting uncontrolled anger eat them alive and the results were deadly.

I later found out that the man with the gun was an Iraqi and a former member of the Saddam Hussein regime. He and others were taking Saddam's money and traveling to neighboring countries and partying. But, ANGER quickly stopped that party.

The next verse says, ***"Do not lie to one another, since you have put off the old man (person) with his practices."*** Col. 3:9.

Being a *"new creation"* in Christ means leaving the practices of your old life...the practices of worldliness behind. Like Lazarus, leave the old clothes of death in the grave and put on the new clothes that God has given to you in Jesus Christ! We are being told what to leave in the graveyard of sin. We now know what to unpack in our lives.

Sinful sexual practices and thoughts. Greed...Anger and lies, lies, lies! You don't need them. They are a result of the Devil having a hold on your life, but, as a Christ-follower, you now are seeking Christ. You want Jesus to have a stronghold on your life. Why? Because you are a new creation in HIM!

CHAPTER SEVEN...
LOOK AT MY NEW CLOTHES

The next statement in our text says, *"...and put on the new man (person), who is being renewed in knowledge according to the image of his Creator."*

The cool thing about this letter is we are not only told what to take out of our lives but, he tells us what to put in its' place. We aren't left wondering. It becomes obvious to us. We can all understand it. It's not rocket science.

I remember being told about...and later actually seeing... churches that had an "N-O" mentality. The teaching and the preaching seemed to always center around what you CAN'T do. I call it a "Can't Do" religion. Remember those churches?
Check the length of your dress.
Check the length of your hair, men.
Too much make-up.
Music is too loud or too fast or too worldly.
Dresses only, no pants...ladies.

I could name many more legalistic restrictions of "Cant's."

One of the things I love about this letter of Colossians chapter three is it tells us things to take out of our lives AND how to replace them.

I don't want to be told continually what NOT to do. Tell me what I CAN DO!

I remember one year leading a team of Americans to several countries in Eastern Europe. One Sunday we divided into teams and left to go to several churches. My father and I visited a church together. It was packed with people downstairs and in the balcony.

It was normal for there to be multiple sermons in one service. So my father preached the first message and I shared the final message. When the worship was near conclusion a leader in the church stepped to the pulpit and reminded the congregation that my father and I were real believers. The previous Sunday they had some American preachers visit. He told the congregation that those preachers were **not** true believers. The reason he gave was the speakers from the previous Sunday preached with their suit coats unbuttoned while preaching and my father and I kept our suit coats buttoned while preaching!

UNBELIEVABLE! Can you find that dress code in the Bible?

Okay...here we go. *"Therefore, God's chosen ones, holy and beloved, put on heartfelt compassion, kindness, humility, gentleness, and patience..."* v. 12.

Some versions of the Bible say, *"The Elect of God..."* This word, "Elect" has caused a lot of controversy over the years with church scholars and church fathers. My wish is that we could *"Reason together"* without arguing and fighting. Our mission is a much higher calling than disputing with one another. We should realize our critical work of getting the Gospel to everyone. That's where our time and energy need attention. Praise God for allowing us to be a part of His Elect.

But, whatever you believe about "Election" pales in the light of the fact that God has called us to take His Gospel to ALL nations and to ALL people!

Therefore, we are a part of God's family. Plain and simple. As a part of God's family, we need to be "Holy." Peter quoted the Old Testament when he said to remember that God said *"...you are to be holy in all your conduct; for it is written, 'Be holy, because I am holy.'"* **1 Peter 1:15-16.**

You show your love for Christ and your holy living by showing compassion to others. "Heartfelt" compassion. Don't just give someone food, but, show them that they are important to you as well.

Care for them. Go the extra mile for them. Go back and give again and again. Make sure they know that your concern and compassion for them is genuine.

Go beyond what others do. All the terms used in this verse are relational.

This is what we do in our relationships with people. We have *"Compassion, kindness, humility, gentleness, and patience."*

I know that your *"kindness, gentleness, and patience"* can be put to a test often.

I was in Oradea, Romania, one evening with my evangelist friend, Sonny. We had just arrived from Budapest and were new to the city and country. We had arranged to meet a young man named Erhnu. He was twenty years old and spoke English well. He took us to a restaurant in the center of the city for supper. We had to park several blocks away because the down-town streets were closed.

It was a meal like I had never experienced before. We were seated, but before we were seated the waiter removed the tablecloth from the table and shook it out with a snap and flipped it to the reverse side placing it back on the table. Then we were seated. No menus. No ordering. No choices. The number of people was three and the waiter brought out three meals...all the same. It was what everyone ate...so, to stave off hunger we ate what was given.

During the meal, I gave Sonny the money I had exchanged in the hotel prior to leaving for supper. I took out all the Romanian money and gave to Sonny what belonged to him and we both put it into our pockets.

Little did I realize that someone in the restaurant was watching the entire transaction.

When we left the restaurant someone began following us. While walking down the sidewalk a man behind us began speaking. Erhnu told us that he said he wanted all our money. We told him that he was not getting our money. I had my camera strapped to my belt and he said he wanted my camera. I told him that it wasn't going to happen.

Then Erhnu said the man was getting ready to jump us and fight. I looked at Sonny and asked, *"What are we going to do?"* Now, Sonny was the age of my father and a great man of God and I trusted his advice. He had been on several international excursions and I knew his experience would be an advantage for us. Sonny replied to me, *"I'm going to coldcock that sucker!"* Erhnu says, *"He's getting ready to jump you."* So I turned around and he was immediately in my face. I put up my hands to defend myself when suddenly he saw a group of young men across the street and began yelling at them to help him. He told them that we had money and he needed their help to fight us for it.

Erhnu immediately told us to begin running to the car. We had to run approximately six blocks and we reached the car before they reached us. We all got into the car and drove away…quickly!

Put on *"**Compassion, kindness, humility, gentleness and patience.**"*

I am convinced that if they had only given us a chance we would have shown them compassion. That's the reason we were there.
You can think what you want, but Sonny and I loved those guys and spent that evening praying for them.

I challenge you to act upon your compassion and kindness. Bless someone by fulfilling a need in their life. That's kindness. BUT…then do it again and again. That's compassion!

What about the thing called "Humility?" Do you have it? Do you live with it?

My father always said that he wrote the book called, **"Humility and How I Attained It!"**

If you question whether you possess humility...here's a thought. **"Once you think you have it...you just lost it!"**

Humility means you will NOT become short or impatient or resent the ones to whom you are showing kindness. You will forgive and be compassionate.

Look at the next verse in **Colossians 3:13.**
"...accepting one another and forgiving one another if anyone had a complaint against another. Just as the Lord has forgiven you, so also YOU must forgive."

Even if they have complained against you...you forgive them. And, by the way, forgiveness is unlimited. Regardless of the sin...regardless of the transgression...**You Forgive!**

I feel a little like the Apostle Paul at this point. If someone thinks they have a right to complain...I do. Being mistreated is not fun. Being lied about is not something I have always enjoyed. But there have been times...

What about Jesus? Do you think He enjoyed being made fun of and being called the **"Son of the devil?"** I don't think so. What about the disciples...Peter, James and John? They stood at the Temple court day after day speaking about the one these same people had just crucified. They were telling the truth about a Man who could change their lives by simple Faith.

What was the result of them telling the truth? Beatings! Grumblings! Taunting! Prison time!

So, why should I complain? I won't and I will not.

Have you ever noticed that much of the taunting and rebellion comes from the religious sector? Seriously. For Jesus and His disciples, it was from the religious people...at least that's what they had conned people to believe about them. They were the priests, religious teachers, and church leaders. The centuries haven't changed the fact that many people today are the same. It will continue until Jesus returns. In fact, it will worsen.

When you see someone getting "beat up" by gossip and religious arrogance...stop and be a Good Samaritan. Lend a hand. Be an encourager. Be forgiving by looking past the rhetoric and seeing their heart. Most times, the heart is much different than the rhetoric.

Isn't that what God did for you? Seriously, you don't deserve His forgiveness. I don't deserve God's forgiveness.
Remember the Son of God dying the way He did for us?
How could you **ever** think you deserve that kind of forgiveness? I know I don't.
And, He asks us to love other people the way He loved us.
You see, compassion and kindness and humility are emptying ourselves into the life of Jesus Christ and loving people because of Him.
We give up our rights for the rights of God.

We were in Beirut, Lebanon, for our first citywide crusade. The outdoor crusade was in the Christian sector of Beirut.

A short number of years prior to this crusade there had been a civil war in Lebanon between the Christians and the Muslims. Linda, my wife, was with me and they were making sure we had all that we needed.

They had assigned a young man, twenty-five years old, to take care of us during each crusade event. His name was "Sammy." He took care of us well.

One thing I noticed about Sammy was that he was a great servant. He was always in the place where he could help with the work and care for people...a real servant for the Lord. On one occasion I asked about Sammy...what was his story. Sammy was a Palestinian refugee living in a refugee camp in northern Lebanon in the city of Tripoli. He had heard the Gospel of Jesus Christ and by Faith gave his life to Jesus. When his father heard the news, he had Sammy beaten and told him to recant this new Faith. Sammy refused to meet his father's wishes and continued to grow in his Faith. One day Sammy's father had him kidnapped and locked him away in a place in Tripoli.

Sammy's friends had gotten word to him that his father had announced the day and time he would have Sammy executed for turning his back on Islam. The friends broke Sammy out of the prison where he was being held and took him to the Christian sector of Beirut to live with believers. Sammy was a large young man with a huge personality. Everyone loved him. He had a great deal of love for people. His love for God was extremely strong and his life was a testimony of that love. His biggest desire was to see people come to Jesus Christ by Faith. One day Sammy went to a Mosque. He wanted to announce the call to prayer. It is customary for Muslims to have five calls to prayer a day. There is a loudspeaker on the Mosque to announce the call to prayer so people will stop what they are doing and go to the mosque to pray. So, Sammy was allowed to make the call to prayer.

His voice rang out all over that part of the city calling people to prayer. (Sammy told me this story himself). What he did was recite John 3:16...over and over...in Arabic!!! He laughed when telling this story and simply said, *"My people need to know Jesus!"*

Sammy had emptied himself into the life of Jesus Christ and was working for Him. He had given up his rights and had given all the rights to his life to God. That's exactly what God wants from us. Remember, God owns us and has every right in the world to our life and everything in it.

Sammy had forgiven his father. He wanted his father to know Jesus.

Are you curious as to how much you should forgive others? Sammy illustrated that love for us. Even if someone desires to kill you...forgive him! It's the embodiment of how God loves us. So has someone done you wrong? What would Jesus do? He would do what He has taught Sammy to do...Love them. Forgive them. Be kind to them.

The next verse continues this theme.

Read...

***"Above all, put on love—the perfect bond of unity."* V. 14.**

"Above ALL...put on love." More than forgiveness...more than humility...more than kind words...more than a hug...more than acts of kindness...PUT ON LOVE!

Love is larger than all these things. If you do any or all these things without love...you are empty and it is worthless. Love encompasses all the other expressions. Love ties the knot of forgiveness and kindness. To another church, Paul writes, *"...Now these three remain: faith, hope, and love. But the greatest of these is LOVE!"* **1 Corinthians 13:13.**

How are you doing so far? Are you following THE MAP? We have unpacked the old grave clothes of sin and have been instructed what to pack. It's ALL good. It's ALL pleasing to God. It is His will for your life. AND, you know what your parents told you many times...It is **good for you**!
But, this time it is more true than ever.

Let's put on something else. Get ready to pack.

CHAPTER EIGHT...
LET PEACE RULE

"AND let the peace of the Messiah, to which you were also called in one body, control your hearts.
Be thankful." V. 15.

The original language says *"Let the peace FROM Christ... RULE."* *Brabeuto* (Greek)...Let Rule.

I love sports. My wife and I enjoy the game of basketball very much. It seems like you can fall asleep watching some of the other sports games, but basketball is active...continuously moving.

The one sound that rules the basketball game more than any other is the sound of the referee's whistle. When Cleveland won the NBA championship in 2016...I never wanted to hear a whistle blow for a Cleveland infraction. The whistle can control the game. Still, I realize that it needs to control the game. There is a rulebook for basketball. Players must follow the rules for the game so the game will be played fairly. By the way, when the final whistle blew...we were the CHAMPS!

On Monday evenings I host guys in a school gym to play basketball. One year they were playing the game without a referee and making their own calls. But they began to argue frequently about the calls, fouls, rules...and they were wasting a lot of time. So Vince and I decided to referee the games. We would blow whistles when we saw a rule broken.

Sometimes the guys would argue with our calls, but we had the whistles and we were enforcing the rules of the game. They had to go with the call...no questions.

For example, if you possess the ball and you step on the out-of-bounds line...the whistle is blown and the ball is awarded to the opposing team. You broke the rule.

What about the peace of Christ *"ruling"* in your life? If you have put on the new clothes of eternal life in Christ...you need to embody His Peace.

You quit warring against people and exhibit Peace toward them. When things don't go your way, show people that you are different because you have the Peace of God in your life. Having the Peace of Christ is your "calling."

It isn't that you are supposed to have it...it is that you DO have it because God called you to exhibit His Peace!

It means being a Peacemaker.

Truth is revealed through Peace...Hate is revealed through war.

Be a Peacemaker in your home. Don't demand your rights from your spouse.

You are working on becoming "One in Christ" therefore your rights don't apply.

Colossians 3:15 is speaking about the ***"Peace of Messiah."***
It's a Peace that the world knows nothing about. Maybe they talk about peace when two countries are not at war with each other.

They may even call it peace when marriage partners aren't bickering with each other. Some of my family grew up in East St. Louis. I had cousins who thought it was peace when you could walk the streets and not be attacked by one of the "Gangs."

But, the Peace that comes from the Messiah is totally different than the peace known by the world. God's Peace can be exhibited when a person who is a Christ-follower possesses Peace in the middle of trouble. It is the Peace that God gives when the situation around you is not peaceful.

It's a Peace that people in the world rarely see **and** they certainly don't understand it. It's God's Peace.

Look...it's God's Peace that should ***"control your hearts!"***
One Monday night the guys were playing. One of the guys kept coming to me and asking about the way one of the guys was guarding him. He kept saying *"It's wrong!"* I didn't take a stand for either guy, so they kept playing. Then all of a sudden the two young men began yelling at each other.

They grabbed each other and began to brawl. Down on the floor, they went. Both of them had long dreadlocks and so they each pulled the other's hair. They were throwing punches. Finally, I told everyone to go home and told the two guys they needed to stop acting like a couple of big babies. So we left the building and they began fighting again on the blacktop. I took my phone and began dialing 9-1-1 when one of the guys said he was NOT going to jail over this. They both stopped and the fighting was over.

Their squabble looked nothing like God's Peace.
They were mad. Why? I'm convinced that neither one of them were interested in God's Peace at that moment.
They wanted their way. They wanted to impose their way on each other.
Now...that's a snapshot of how the world determines peace.
Beat the snot out of your opponent until they surrender and call it a "Peace Treaty."
Yell at your spouse long enough until they give in and you call it "Peace."
Reprimand your kids until they surrender to your will and call it "Peace."
Lie and gossip until you get a following of some people and call it a "Victory."
Join a protest and walk the city streets and smash and destroy everything you see until you get your way and call it a "Peaceful protest."
THAT'S NOT PEACE!!!

Peace is surrendering to the will of God in your life and in the lives of others involved. Peace is when both you and your enemy can come to God together and find HIS way out. Peace is leaving your will at the altar of sacrifice and allowing God to work His perfect will in and through you.
Peace is doing it God's way...NOT your way.
That's the "Peace of Messiah!"

The Heavenly Referee is blowing His whistle a lot today. Constant fouling between nations and races and marriages and politicians and religions and church members and on and on and on.

A day is coming when God will blow the final whistle. It's called the "Trumpet Sound!"

Until then *"Let the Peace of Messiah...control your hearts."*

During my first visit to Kyiv, Ukraine, we were asked to divide into three groups on the city square in the center of the city to share the Gospel and distribute Bibles to those who would choose to come to Christ by Faith. I remember the scene. There were literally thousands of people walking through the square going in every direction. I had a team with me. I stood on the edge of a concrete wall that was about two feet in height and began to share the Gospel. After about ten minutes I asked all who would like to pray with me and better understand what it means to come to Jesus Christ to step forward and come near me.

The response was great. I took a moment to pray with them and then explained that we had brought a gift to give to them. The gift was a Bible that had been translated into Russian. I did not expect what took place next.

At that time the black market was at its peak. Young men with gym bags hanging around their shoulders began descending on us by great numbers. What I had not known until then was that the Bibles we were giving away would bring good money on the open market...the Black Market. They were taking all the Bibles they could for their personal profit.

People began shoving each other to get a Bible. People were knocked to the ground and stepped on so they could get a Bible. Our Bibles were in boxes and hands were reaching into those boxes grabbing as many Bibles as they could. There was a wall on one side of the square and one of our team members was pinned against that wall with a box of Bibles in his hands yelling for help. He said, *"Somebody help me. I can't breathe!"* Those of us who saw him told him to throw the box into the crowd so they would no longer press on him. He did and he was relieved of the crowd pressure and ran for his life. In fact, all of us ran for our lives. Our bus was parked a couple of blocks away and we simply yelled for all the team to go to the bus as quickly as possible. When we got to the bus the driver closed the door behind us. We noticed people running behind us to get more Bibles.

While sitting on the bus one of our team members was sitting across from me attempting to readjust his glasses that had been badly bent out of shape. I asked him what had happened. He told me that his glasses had been stepped on. Then he said, *"Don, they were on my face when they got stepped on!"*

Aside from the Black Market guys, I had never seen such a hunger for the Word of God.

It was a result of people in a nation that did not allow the Bible to be a part of their culture. These were the same Socialist/ Communist leaders who believed that there was no God and did not permit their people to seek after Him and worship Him. (I'm praying that America never devolves to such paganism).

Certainly, there was no peace on the streets of Kyiv that day.
It is true what someone has said:
"NO GOD NO PEACE...KNOW GOD KNOW PEACE!"
Beware America. These same leanings are in our culture today.
Stand against it!

CHAPTER NINE...
NO PLACE LIKE HOME

"Let the Word of Christ DWELL in you in all wisdom." V. 16.

The word *"Dwell"* is the key to this statement. I live in my house. I could call it my dwelling place. In the Greek language...the language in which this letter was originally written... the word is:

ἐνοικέω (en-oy-keh'-o).

The literal meaning of this word is to dwell at home or inhabit. (Strong's Concordance).

Therefore, the proper place for the Word of God or the words of Christ is in your life. There is something that accompanies the word of Christ. It is extremely important in this context. *"Let the word of Christ dwell IN you in all WISDOM!"*

I'm just a simple guy and it looks like to me that apart from the Word of God and/or the word of Christ in your life...there is NO wisdom. Is that what it looks like to you? It does to me. The Word of God needs to be *"at home"* in your life. It needs to feel at home in your life. It seems to me that so many people make the Word of God feel like a stranger in their lives. It's not important enough to give it a *"home"* in their lives.

Again, being a simple guy I think about what it means for me to be in my home.

When I am home, I am comfortable.

I do whatever I want. It's MY home. If I want to hang my coat on the doorknob…I do it. If I kick off my shoes and let them lay where they land…I do it (until my wife tells me to pick them up). Prediabetes days I loved Snickers candy bars. We even named our first poodle dog "Snickers." My wife, Linda, knew how much I loved Snickers candy bars. But she was always trying to limit my intake of these scrumptious bars. One day she came home with the groceries. I noticed that she had bought a six-pack of Snickers bars. I simply noticed. No big deal…Right? The next day I came home from work and she was not there. The thought came to my mind that the only one home is me and six Snickers bars. I went to the place she always keeps the bars. But, something was different. They were NOT there. *"Oh my,"* I thought. *"Where are they?"* I looked in every nook in the kitchen and the bars were nowhere to be found. At this point, I knew she had hidden them from me. I had determined that I was going to find them. This is my house and I can search any-where and everywhere I desire.

No limits.

I searched in all the closets. I looked under all the beds. I went through all the drawers and closets in the kids' rooms. I thought I had searched every place. *"Where could she have hidden them?"* I thought.

But...no, it couldn't be...I found them stashed in her dresser under her underwear!!! Yep...this is my house and I dwell in this place and I can even go there!

Well, to bring this event to an end...I sat down with a full glass of cold milk and had a feast with SIX SNICKERS BARS!

During my life, I have visited many homes to eat a meal with the pastors of churches where I am speaking. I have noticed that many times when we arrive the host family will tell us to *"Just make yourselves at home."*

As I reflect on that gesture of kindness I am curious if they're really serious. Does that mean I can go through their closets... Go through the kitchen cabinets and drawers...look under their beds...go through their underwear drawers? That's what I do at my home!?!?

NO! I have figured it out. What they really mean is, *"You sit down and don't you move until I call you to eat!!!"*

Look...the Word of God and the words of Christ need to be at home in your life. It needs to dwell in you. It needs to go under the bed of your life. It needs to be in the closets of your life. It needs to be in every drawer in your life. **AT HOME!!!**

Do you desire wisdom? Let God's Word live in you. Let it feel comfortable in every part of your life. You cannot be wise until God's Word is at home in you. You cannot teach without the Word of God being at home in your life.

I have news for you. You may have gone far in your education process with more degrees than a thermometer hanging on your wall, but, your wisdom only comes from God's Holy Word being at home in your life.

When God's Word is at home in your life...all is well.

It will put a song in your heart.

You will know that God is doing wonderful things in you and you will naturally have a desire to give God gratitude and glory.

Don't forget that one tiny word...Dwell. It is a key to THE MAP in your life. It's what makes your life home for God's Word.

It's what puts a song in your heart.

It is the key to you being "wise".

It's a way to make you look like, act like, talk like, think like, and be what God intended for you to be.

Read it daily. Learn from it. Pack it in your life.

"Hide it in your heart that you may NOT sin against God!" **Psalm 119:11.**

Then you are to use what you have learned from God's Word... being at home in your life, to *"...teach and admonish one another in all wisdom..."* (v. 16). "Teaching..." That is telling others what you have learned from God's Word.

"Admonishing...That is advising or urging others to learn from God's Word and act upon it. It is learning from it and applying the messages that are coming from God's Word.

Don't just read it...DO IT!

Don't just say the words...ACT UPON IT!

Don't just skim it...SOAK IT IN!

"Admonish" also means to share the warnings that are given in God's Word. What warning?

In Colossians Paul also writes,
"We proclaim Him, WARNING AND TEACHING EVERYONE WITH ALL WISDOM, so that we may present everyone mature in Christ." **1:28.**

He is saying again what he has already stated.
"Warn and teach everyone in all wisdom!"
Wisdom comes from letting God's Word be at home in your life, then, applying it. Teaching His Word so other people will know what God desires for them.
Do it, my friend, and it will cause changes in your life. Look at what he says. *"...singing psalms, hymns, and spiritual songs, with gratitude in your hearts to God!"*
3:16.

You may already know how and where to begin reading God's Word. Or you may want to know where and how to begin reading your Bible? Your pastor and/or mentor can assist you on how and where to begin. My suggestion would be, to begin with, the book of John...the Gospel of John. It is refreshing to read the life of Jesus and the heartfelt stories that John tells. Then read some of Paul's letters. Galatians, Ephesians, Philippians, and Colossians.
Make sure you read James' letter. James was the half-brother of Jesus. By all means...get started as quickly as you can and stick with it daily!

Letting God's Word dwell in you will put a song in your life. It will cause you to express joy and happiness like never before. It will give you confidence that has alluded you all your life.

When you allow God's Word to dwell in you...to be at home in you...you will have more confidence in the life you're living for Christ.

Christ-followers should **not** be walking around with doubt and fear and a lack of knowing where they are going or what they are to do.

They need confidence that God is directing them and leading them.

They **do not** need to walk around like they've been *"sucking butter out of a churn"* with long faces that express fear and failure.

Come on, where is the *"Joy of the Lord"* in your life? Your life becomes a picture that says, *"I'm a loser and the Devil's got a hold of my life!"*

That's ALL about to change. Get into God's Word. Let it *"Dwell"* in your life. Read it so much that it becomes a living fire in you.

It will change how you look.

It will give you wisdom.

It will give you confidence.

It will give you JOY!

One day I took a team of ministers to Ukraine to lead a three-day Pastor's Conference. There were over sixty local and regional pastors who attended. We had a great time. We would lead four seminars each day. Many of the pastors were older and had some great stories to tell.

It seemed like every day the pastors would come to the conference with great joy.

Their facial expressions and their actions showed us how much they loved God and how totally committed they were to His service.

But, on the third day, something changed. The meeting was to begin at 9:00 AM. As the men walked into the room there was a sadness on their faces.

Someone began to sing a song in a minor key that was very dark while others joined in to sing. I asked our interpreter what was the problem. She told me that several years ago during WWII on this day there was a great massacre in their country. The enemy had come into their country and taken all the land and killed many of their fathers, mothers, grandfathers, etc. One pastor told how as a small child he watched troops enter their home and toss the children out while locking their parents inside their home and setting it on fire. He watched as his parents were killed in that fire.

This day was called "A Day of Mourning" throughout the country.

I was extremely saddened by the stories these men told concerning their families and friends during the war. But, I am reminded how they were there, in the conference, learning more about God's Word and doing all they could to learn so they could teach His Word to others with wisdom!

The looks on their faces of joy and expectation were contagious for all of us who taught that week.

I'm reminded of how they had spent years without God's Word. The government had forbidden anyone from possessing a Bible. So, they would sneak a Bible into a community and remove the pages.

Then, families would take the page that they had been given and copy by hand the words and pass that page to someone else so they could receive another page and copy it. This took place for years under Socialism...a government that is led by people who say that there is no God and follow humanistic leadership.

But, the doors opened in those Socialistic countries and we found millions of people who knew God's Word and had the joy of God in their lives.

I met a team of believers in the country of Hungary. A few days before going we had shipped 35,000 Bibles and several Bible commentaries for pastors and teachers translated into their own language to Budapest so we could give them to Romanian believers. The communist leaders of Romania had announced that guests to their country were not allowed to bring Bibles. Along with the Bibles we also shipped humanitarian goods such as clothing, etc.

I visited the Romanian Consulate in Budapest to receive a document proving we were allowed to bring the humanitarian goods. I received the document that I needed.

We left the next day for Romania. Our team divided into three groups and we traveled in three separate vans. After about 150 miles we arrived at the Hungarian/Romanian border. We were deep into the forest. All the border guards were carrying AK-47 rifles while checking every vehicle. We passed through the Hungarian border guards with no problem. We then moved on to the Romanian border guards. It was obvious to all of us that they were more curious about why we were going into their country. They inspected every vehicle with more intensity.

Each one of our vans had boxes of Bibles and Bible commentaries covered with the humanitarian goods.

Yes, we were taking the Bibles without the Romanian government permission! The year prior to this we had shipped 75,000 Bibles to the Soviet Union. At that time, they too announced that every person entering their country was allowed only one Bible to take with them.

On this occasion in Romania, we had covered our Bibles with clothing, etc.

Our vans were inspected one at a time.

We were praying that they would **not** demand that we pull everything out of the vans. The first van got through without a problem. The same was true of the second van. Then, the van in which I was riding was asked to pull forward for inspection. The driver of our van was a young man, twenty years old, named Blaze. Blaze and I got out of our van and carefully watched the inspectors. They asked us to open the back door of the van. I opened it while Blaze stood nearby. When I opened it I noticed the boxes had shifted and the clothing had moved off one of the boxes. On the side of the box was written the word Bible in the Romanian translation. When I saw it...I immediately closed the rear door.

Blaze had also seen the box. The guard, carrying his AK-47 stepped toward the van. Immediately Blaze got his guitar which was laying in the van...grabbed the guard's coat sleeve and asked him if he liked music. The guard was distracted by Blaze and his music and walked away from the van to listen to Blaze. As fast as I could I closed the door and asked the driver to pull the van forward to get the van out of the inspection lane.

Our papers were all stamped and approved and we were allowed to leave the border and travel on into Romania. By the way, we were entering into the area of Romania that is commonly called "Transylvania." All I knew about Transylvania was that Frankenstein lived there.

We journeyed approximately five miles when we arrived at our destination city...Oradea.

When we got to the church where they were waiting for us I met the pastor who was waiting on the street for our arrival. The first thing he told me is that members of the church were inside praying for us. He asked me if we had any problems at the border. I assured him that all was good and he was extremely relieved. He then told me that a friend of his from Russia was attempting to bring 6,000 Bibles to them by crossing at the same border crossing. He told me that three weeks ago his friend came with a car loaded with the Bibles. The border guard found the Bibles and turned him away. A few days later he came with another car where he had put the Bibles in every hidden place he could in the vehicle, but they again found the Bibles.

The pastor then tells me that the guards became angry that he had tried a second time. The guards took his friend into the woods at the border crossing and killed him.

He said that incident has caused believers to pray for your safety in crossing the border.

God's Word is a powerful book. It is a book that is changing lives all over the world.

It can change your life. Read it. Learn from it. Apply its' message to your life. Don't treat it like a motel key where you check it in on Sunday morning and check it out at noon!

Let God's Word be at home in your life. Let it be a daily source of nourishment for your life.

Today, in America, we have no excuse for lacking the joy and the confidence that God is in control. Let your face show it. Let your life live it by being a reflection of God's Word.

CHAPTER TEN...
DO EVERYTHING FOR HIM

LOOK AT VERSE SEVENTEEN

"And whatever you do, in word or deed, do everything in the name of the Lord Jesus, giving thanks to God the Father through Him." v. 17

One day, while in the former Soviet Union, I was asked to go to a hospital that had been built deep in the forest so few would find it. The Socialist government leaders desired to hide their activity of wickedness. You see, the people that were sent to this place were sent there to die. They had a disease that was curable in many parts of the world, but, for some reason, the leaders would rather let them die than to purchase the medication for their survival.

We were driven as far as we could go by car. Then we proceeded to walk the remainder of the journey. We walked through a heavily wooded area for about two miles. On the way, we came to a large clearing in the woods. The cleared area looked to be about the size of a football field. We stopped and our interpreter told us about this clearing. During WWII the Nazi military cleared this area to bring Jewish people to be murdered, burned, and then buried. The clearing was at one time a huge hole that had been dug to bury the people who had been killed. The hole was open for approximately ten months. After ten months the hole was filled in and another place was prepared for their dastardly work. I asked our interpreter if she knew how many people were killed at this place. She said that she had been told that approximately 50,000 people were murdered and buried in that hole.

I remember pondering for a few moments the reality of standing on the grave of 50,000 people!

We then moved on to the hospital where there were one hundred and four patients that had been sent there to die. One lady, twenty-four years old had just arrived the day before. We stood at a distance and God gave me the opportunity to share the Gospel of Jesus Christ. Some prayed to receive eternal life that day.

I will never forget that experience.

I will especially remember the grave of 50,000 people who died at the hands of Socialist dictators thirsting for power and wealth at the expense of the lives of precious people. A power-hungry group of people who tell people there is no God and the Bible is a book of stories and myths and cannot be trusted.

This kind of thought has infiltrated our world.

Some of its' godless thinking has even crossed the borders of America and is poisoning people here...good and bad.

When Colossians says for us **"...*to do everything in the name of the Lord Jesus...*"** it is empowering us to do the will of God and seek Him in **all** things so that we will receive from Him all that He has for us!

When God gives...it is greater than we could ever think or imagine. Therefore, when all that we do in word or deed is done for God's Glory...we give Him "Thanks."

The believer needs to live his/her entire life to give God glory. It is important.

For several years I had the joy of leading evangelistic meetings in the city of Beirut, Lebanon. One year we were planning an outdoor meeting in July in the Christian sector of Beirut. The city is divided into two divisions...Christian and Muslim.

It was an election year and one of their popular leaders had been assassinated by a planted car bomb.

In the spring of that year, I was in Eastern Europe for conferences and a crusade. I received a call from my wife who told me that our team leaders in Lebanon had asked if I could go there as soon as possible. We were able to make the arrangements so I left Poland and arrived in Beirut. I was taken to meet with several political leaders who were running for a political seat in the Lebanese government. Most of the leaders were Muslim, but, every time I asked them for permission to close our meeting in prayer...they agreed. It was really cool! I knew God had planned this trip.

Then arrangements were made for me to visit a Catholic Monastery in the mountains surrounding Beirut. One of the Cardinals of the Catholic church lived in that Monastery. He had been invited by our president to visit the White House for a personal meeting. I was invited to attend his final mass before he left for America. Following the mass, I was taken to a room where he would be coming to hold a news conference. They placed me in the chair next to the Cardinal so that I was certain to have a conversation with him. He eventually came and sat next to me. We engaged in conversation for approximately ten minutes. He spoke English well. We talked about our work and his upcoming visit to America to meet our president and then we shook hands and I was taken out of the room so his news conference could begin.

On the way back to our hotel one of the media guys who was riding with us received a phone call. Of course, I did not understand the conversation, but he paused for a moment and asked me if I would be willing to meet with the president of Lebanon the next day. I thought he was kidding so I made light of his request. Then the tone got serious. He said I am on the phone with someone from the president's office, he saw you on television with the Cardinal and would like to meet with you. So, the next day we went to the White House of Lebanon.

After meeting with the president for approximately forty-five minutes, he asked me a question. *"What can I do for you?"* Our crusade director was with me and we immediately told him we would be leading an evangelistic event in Beirut in July. I asked, *"Would you make it possible for us to hold this event in the central part of Beirut?"* He assured me that he would make that possible. He assigned to us seventy-five of his special troops to watch over the area while we were there.

It was unbelievable! Over 4,000 people attended each night for five nights. Hundreds of people came to Jesus by Faith, including the son of one of the former presidents.

"Whatever you do...do everything in the name of the Lord Jesus giving thanks to God the Father through Him!"
v. 17.

We will revisit this subject in the finale of this book because the final verse of this chapter reemphasizes our intentions in what we do and say.

CHAPTER ELEVEN...DON'T MESS WITH GOD'S PLAN

Therefore, before our conclusion, the writer has some things to say concerning members of the household. God gives His plan in the building of the home structure.
Remember...this is God's plan. It's part of THE MAP! No man can do this. No woman would allow him! Ha! Ha!

My grandfather told me many times that he was the head of his home. But, he quickly added that my grandmother was the "neck" that turns the head! Ha, Ha again!

When Christ is in your home...you will pay close attention to the structure that He gives. The home was created by God and He knows the best way for it to function.
We are **not** at liberty to change God's structure. We all know what happens when we mess with what God has created.
IT MAKES A MESS!!! So, here it is.

"Wives, be submissive to your husbands, as is fitting in the Lord."
Colossians 3:18

Like the organized structure of the military, there is an organized structure for the home. No Private attempts to usurp the position of the General without dire consequences. There have been attempts by many people to usurp the position that God has given in the structure of the home. In fact, the results of such activity are all around us. In America, the deterioration of the structure of the home has devastated much of the physical and moral fiber of our nation.

The ONLY remedy for this mess is to go back to God's way... God's original structure...and leave our gerrymandering out of it.

What about that word *"Submit?"* This is referring to position, not person.

Again, like in the military. A private may be gifted far more than the General, but, as someone said, he/she *"doesn't submit to a General because they are smarter but because they are the General."*

God has placed the order of the structure of the home as the Husband, Wife, and Children. (Sorry, but, all pets have been left out of this structure).

Well, I am similar to many men in our world. I am married and we have children.

Therefore, I am fully aware of how this structure operates. I realize that God has given to me a responsibility in the structure of my home.

I am the husband. I am the father. I have responsibilities that have **not** been given to my wife.

Likewise, she has responsibilities that have NOT been given to me.

I must be honest, the older I get the more I know that my responsibility is to love my wife with all my heart. AND, loving her requires me to rethink my responsibilities toward her.

My responsibility is NOT to lord over her.

My responsibility is NOT to add to her load by creating more burdens for her.

My responsibility is NOT to watch her become weary with whatever life throws at her.

My responsibility is to LOVE her. Do you know what that means? It means to help carry her load. Be strong in character. Be faithful to her. I am to make her **know** that I love her more than anything in this world. It's not something that is easily done with only words.

Love is an emotion of action. The Bible says to *"Carry one another's burdens; in this way, you will fulfill the law of Christ."* **Gal. 6:2.**

As a husband...be a gentleman. Open the door for her. Help carry the groceries into the house. Help clean the house. God gave wives, **not** to be a doormat but to be our partner...Our NUMBER ONE partner.

So, for many ladies, the act of "Submission" is a terrible thought. For many, the word is out-of-touch and antiquated. It is a word for wives of old...NOT the twenty-first century.

You didn't ask for it, but, the following are some thoughts I have concerning *"wives being submissive to their husbands."*

1. "Submission" does NOT mean the wife is inferior to her husband.
2. Knowing the true meaning of the word...how God intended to define it will cause wives to **desire** to be obedient to God's will.
3. When a husband loves his wife as God intended...he will make the act of submission a positive action and not a negative action or reaction. It is the responsibility of the husband to create an atmosphere in their marriage where his wife feels like she is loved and cherished. She needs to know that her husband sees her as someone worth much more than gold.
4. Wives...back to being obedient to God. When you rid yourself of the "Women's Rights" attitude and rebellion due to selfish desires and improper attention... THEN you will begin to understand what it means to have a heart like God. Seriously, God created marriage as something fun and enjoyable.
5. Don't be offended so easily at your husband.
6. Don't criticize your husband.
7. Don't nag your husband.
8. Don't compare your husband or your marriage with someone else.
9. Submission is a two-way street. **Both** husbands and wives are expected to submit to God...In everything!
10. Pray together. Love together. Talk together. Stay together.

Wives being submissive to their husbands means they are being obedient to God's well-organized blueprint for the home.

Now, for the home to run like a well-oiled machine, the husband will need to execute the role of the husband according to God's blueprint.

"Husbands, love your wives, and don't be bitter against them."
Colossians 3:19.

"Don't be bitter." To be honest, men, some guys who came before us have given the *"husband"* a bad rap.
Seriously, even in the first century, there is a hint that husbands were bitter. It's an indication that husbands may have mistreated their wives.
Now, you may think that some husbands have given their wives reasons to be bitter. It is possible that a husband may feel justified in being bitter toward his wife...BUT...it is NOT justified. The idea is that loving your wife crosses all boundaries. Even if she is unlovable...don't be bitter. The one instruction given to husbands is to NOT BE BITTER TOWARD THEIR WIVES!

Why have men been given the tag of being a *"Bear?"* One lady asked her friend if she woke up grumpy in the mornings. She replied, *"No, I just let him sleep!"*

In another letter that Paul wrote, he said, **"Husbands, love your wives, just as also Christ loved the church and gave himself for her."**
Ephesians 5:25

So, we are to love our wives just like Christ loved the church? How much did He love the church? He died for the church. He laid down His life for the church. He gave his ALL for the church. Like I said earlier...**Love** is an emotion of **Action**.
The action Christ exemplified for the church is no more and no less what we are to give for our wives.

It's all a matter of **Action**. Don't just tell your wife...show her.

One Sunday morning while in my hotel in Moscow, Russia there were a couple of brothers from the underground church who met us in the lobby. They were going to take us to their church that had been under persecution for many years. I had no idea where we were going because each week the meeting place changed so that they could hide their location from the government. We rode in a van to the outskirts of Moscow and then began to walk.
We walked into the forest for over an hour. At one point I remember crossing a railroad track. Finally, after nearly two hours of traveling and walking in the forest, I heard music. The more we walked the louder the music could be heard. Then, we came upon an opening in the forest and I saw children sitting on the branches in the trees. Someone told me that there were approximately 1500 people there worshipping the Lord! They appropriately called this church, *"The Church in the Forest."*
It was an awesome sight and an unforgettable experience. I watched them sing. I watched them as the pastors spoke from God's Word.

But, I noticed something strange. Most of us were standing, but, in the front row, people had brought small folding stools for the elderly ladies to sit. I noticed those ladies both smiling as well as tears rolling down their faces. I asked my interpreter why they were crying.

She told me that many of these people had never seen Americans and they were glad we were here. But, she said many of these ladies witnessed their husbands being taken by the KGB and forced to go to prisons because of their Faith. And, some of these ladies saw soldiers put guns to the heads of their husbands and sons. They were told to deny Christ or be killed. Because of their love for the Savior...they were killed in the presence of their wives.

Their husbands were examples of "Love in Action."
That is exactly what it means to love your wife and have a good attitude toward her.
We all know that a wife can cause a husband to react and be bitter. Here is the secret to God's blueprint for the marriage.

When, you as a wife, submit to God totally and submit to your husband as an act of obedience to God and His plan for your marriage...
AND...
When, you as a husband, love your wife just as God asked and turn away from ALL bitterness and anger and be willing to love totally and take ACTION, thusly...
You will have accomplished what God's blueprint lays out for you to have a blessed, wonderful, loving, forgiving, relationship that you will be proud to call your marriage!

Spouses are like owning a Cadillac. The better you treat it the better it will treat you.

If it's dirty...wash it. Change the oil regularly. Grease the joints. Repair the rust. Be gentle.

Be loyal to it. Don't be looking to trade her for another. Believe me, she will know. If her battery gets weak, charge her up. Keep her tuned. If she begins to spit and sputter...take her somewhere so she can be reenergized.

Again, be good to her and she will be good to you!

"Children, obey your parents in everything, for this is pleasing to the Lord." **Colossians 3:20**

As long as a child lives under their parent's roof, eats their food, sleep in their house...they are under God's direction to **"obey your parents in everything."** Obviously, when the child has grown and begins their own household...they are no longer under this obligation.

The scripture is filled with the message for children to **"Obey their parents"** and for children to **"Honor your father and mother."**

Ephesians 6:1-3 says, *"Children, obey your parents in the LORD, for this is right. 'Honor your father and mother'-which is the first commandment with a promise- 'so that it may go well with you and that you may enjoy long life on the earth.'"*

There are over a hundred verses I could list where the Bible tells children to love, honor, respect, obey...their parents.

Look, kids, young and old, your parents are a gift to you. Your mom didn't get pregnant with you and God said, *"Uh-Oh...I didn't mean for that to happen."* You were born as a gift to your parents, on purpose, AND you were given parents as a gift to YOU!

Seriously...treat them like God's gifts to you. Help lift the burden they are carrying. Your dad is not your "Old Man" neither is your mom your "Old Lady." They are gifts to you. They love you more than you know.

I have three kids. They all have distinct personalities. They all treat their mother and me differently. We pray for them every day.

When I call my oldest son, I am extremely interested in his home and his ministry. I try not to nag him and I pray for him to be blessed beyond what he could imagine. I pray for his wife and the four grandchildren they have given me. I attempt to find ways to inquire, again, without being a nag.

When I talk to my younger son I am always asking how his work is progressing. I love hearing the details of what he is doing, how his home is doing, and how his son, our grandson, is doing. He is very interested in the political landscape of America. He always has a word of reflection concerning his thoughts about politics.

When I talk to my daughter I am always interested in the activities of her life. As with my sons, her life is filled with activities. She married the greatest son-in-law ever and has two of the greatest little boys you could ever meet. In fact, I feel a bit melancholy for other grandparents knowing that God gave to

Linda and me the greatest grandkids of all time! My kids. I love them more than words could ever express!

My parents were extremely important to me.
My father led me to Faith in Jesus Christ. My mother taught me every sport that I know. She was the "tom-boy" in our family. For fifty years my father was a pastor. The older I became the more respect I had for my parents.
I remember my father's respect for his father.
He, too, was a pastor and a tenant farmer. He raised nine children and had several grandchildren. Whenever we visited my grandparents my father would get his father and ride around the country for most of the day just to be alone with him. He wanted to be with him. He wanted to spend time with him. They were best friends. The day we buried him I remember what my father said to my brother and me. We drove to the cemetery and my father turned to look at my brother and me in the back seat of our car and he said, *"I hope you will be able to bury me with just half of the respect I have for my father."* Years later when my father died his wish came true.
I respected my father so much.
For my brother and me...he was our best friend and our respect for him could not have been greater.

God is looking for us to love and respect our parents. This is another point of action. Your parents will not know your respect for them until you put it on display.

"Fathers, do NOT provoke your children, so they won't become discouraged." Colossians 3:21

You know, when your children see you as a younger parent... you may make some wrong decisions. I know by experience. My parents were in the same boat. My parents married young. I was born on my father's twenty-first birthday. Mom had just turned seventeen when I was born. I was raised by young parents.

With all that energy as a young parent, it may be easy to make decisions that were not good. I did. But the older I became the more I realized those mistakes and how much I needed to correct them.

I was disciplined firmly. As a result, I may have carried on similar discipline to my children. I know today that this is where we need to be careful. We want our children to do right and be as good as they can be. We want them to aspire in their life. But, we need to put on the fruit of patience to raise our children in a loving home so they will not be discouraged when they enter the age of making their own home. Love and discipline. I know it's a challenge. But, God can make it happen.

Just as children should love their parents, we, as parents need to love our children and protect our children and give them all the encouragement we can give. I love my kids. They are the most wonderful children in the world. Love your kids!!!

Our evangelistic work in Eastern Europe included providing programs for children who lived in orphanages. The orphanages in these countries are filled to capacity with wonderful children. Many Americans traveled with me to these cities and they often visited with the children in the orphanages. One day a brother in our group was taken to visit the children in an orphanage. Approximately 300 children were living there. When he spoke to them he noticed that none of the children had shoes. When he asked about their shoes he was told that there was not enough money provided by the government for the children to have shoes. He asked to be taken to the city market where he proceeded to purchase 300 pairs of children's shoes. He was taken back to the orphanage and the workers gave each child a pair of shoes.

When all the shoes had been given to the children...he noticed one child had not received a pair of shoes. He asked to be taken back to the market to purchase shoes for this child. His driver told him that the crusade will begin shortly and Don Betts will be looking for you. He told his driver that he has heard Don Betts speak many times and he will not be disappointed if I miss this one time to purchase this child a pair of shoes. He was correct!

On another occasion, I visited a city in Ukraine during Orthodox Christmas week...the first week in January. We had sent shoeboxes filled with presents from people in America. There were so many children that we had to divide the event into two days. What I had discovered is that many of the parents of the children came to see their children receive the gifts. I asked why the children did not live with their parents. I was told that the parents lived in the country and could not afford to raise their children so they gave them to the orphanage so the government could raise them. Another result of a Socialist government seeking to take more from us to have more for themselves. I pray America will stop the train that is pulling us in that direction. It's subtle, but it's absolute!

We gave gifts to 2,000 children during that event.

I came away from that event thankful for my children and for what we have been given by God. It is not the government's responsibility to raise our kids. God gave that responsibility to parents.

We are to love them.

We are to raise them.

We are to train them.

We are to teach them right from wrong.

We are to nurse them when they are ill.

We are to teach them how much God loves them.

It is OUR responsibility...NOT someone else AND especially NOT the government. Government...stay out of our lives and let us obey God with our families.

Don't make ridiculous demands. Don't be critical of them in any way. They know by your actions if you love them. When you give them unconditional love...they will respond in kind.

Love your children. Get rid of all bitterness. Right, the wrong and be an encourager.

CHAPTER TWELVE...
WHO IS YOUR REAL BOSS

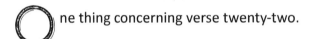ne thing concerning verse twenty-two.

"Slaves, obey your human masters in everything. Don't work only while being watched, in order to please men, but work wholeheartedly, fearing the Lord." 3:22

It is God's will that you respect your boss.
This is another authority structure that God has given. Employees are under the authority of their bosses.
BUT, remember this when you are working.
Have you ever tried to get away with something because you thought the boss wouldn't see you?
WHAT ARE YOU THINKING?!?!
GOD IS ALWAYS WATCHING!!!
When you work, you should **not** be considering whether the boss is looking or not, but, you should be **knowing** that the BIG BOSS...GOD IS WATCHING!
This activity is childishness. It's something you should already know. God is watching. Work hard because you are working as if God was signing your paychecks.

We don't work to please men, rather we work to please God. Sincerely.

The final verses sum it all up.

"Whatever you do, do it enthusiastically, as something done for the Lord and not for men, knowing that you will receive the reward of an inheritance from the Lord—you serve the Lord Christ. For the wrongdoer will be paid back for whatever wrong he has done, and there is NO favoritism." Vv. 23-25

In God's eyes, everything will be done right.
People will be paid back for what kind of workers they become.
Everything will be fair. No human judges...ONLY GOD!

CHAPTER THIRTEEN...
LET'S PRAY

Well, that covers about everything and everyone. This is what I love about this chapter.
Some stuff needs to be taken out of our lives, unpacked, and he names what it is.
Then, he tells us how to replace it...What to pack!

At the close of this book, I ask you to take the prayer challenge. Seriously, it works. I'll give you THE MAP Jesus gave for praying. Matthew 6:6.

"But when you Pray, go into your private room, SHUT YOU DOOR, and Pray to your Father who is in secret.
And your Father who sees in secret will reward you."

1. Go into your Private Room... (with Pen and Paper) Shut the Door
2. God will be there with you
3. Pray
4. Listen to God
5. Be Blessed by God and Go

Seeking what is above begins with seeking God...Personally... Alone...In private! You do not and cannot have worldly distractions around you while you are seeking God.

"Shut the Door." This is the plan Jesus gave.

HERE'S THE PRAYER MAP: (SIMPLIFIED)

Take a blank piece of paper and pen into the room with you and close the door. Get down before God...I prefer on my knees or sometimes just sit alone on the floor.

Ask God to reveal anything in your life that He is doesn't approve.

THEN, LISTEN! Don't talk...just listen.

This part is extremely important. Whatever comes to your mind...write it on the paper.

Whether you agree with it or not...write it down. Things that will come to your mind may surprise you. You may think, *"That's not that bad."* Believe me, if it came to your mind, **God wants you to do something about it.**

He'll bring up relationships that need to be repaired.

He'll bring up attitudes He thinks you need to adjust. Anything that bothers God, may be brought to your mind.

WRITE IT DOWN!

Give yourself at least forty-five minutes to an hour to listen to God. Your prayer life may have been **you** doing all of the talking without allowing God to speak in response. **Give Him time!**

Then, look over your list. Go over each item you have written and one-by-one ask God to show you what to do about it. Write His response next to each item. He'll bring his answer to your mind. Write it down.

Then, commit to doing what God has asked you to do. It may mean a phone call. It may mean a personal visit to someone. It may mean asking someone to forgive you. Whatever it is... just do it!

When you have finished...this should take no less than an hour...Pray and ask God to forgive you for all the things listed on your sheet of paper. Then write **"1 John 1:9"** across the entire paper and claim its' promise.
"If we confess our sins,
He is faithful and righteous to forgive us our sins
and to cleanse us from ALL unrighteousness!"

Now, you can open the door of your Prayer Closet and go live your life...forgiven!

THAT, my friend, is how you *"Seek what is above..."* and *"Set your minds on what is above and NOT on what is on the earth!"*

Are you ready? Now do it!

CONCLUSION...
A LITTLE DIALOGUE...?

YOU: Okay, Betts...NOW what do I do?

ME: Are you serious? You don't know what to do? Let's begin with an inventory of your life—as stated in Colossians 3.

YOU: Okay.

ME: First, are you seeking God every day in your life? **(Vv. 1-4)**

YOU: (Your answer...)

ME: Let's take care of the sin in your life. I'm not judging...we **all** have sin in our lives. You need to *"put to death"*...unpack your sin. So...obvious perpetual sin that you are purposely hiding in your life AND/OR sin that may **not** be obvious to you that is making God unhappy with your life. **(Read vv. 5-9)**

*Now it's time to set aside an hour from your life and go somewhere PRIVATELY to do business with God. Before you

begin, go back to the "HERE'S THE MAP" section (Chapter 13)
and follow the steps for Personal Cleansing.
Don't shortcut this step in your life. It is critical in your relationship with God.

YOU: I did it.
I'm finished. That was amazing!

ME: Now, how are you going to live as the *"New Person"* that
God has given to you? **(Read vv. 10-14)**

YOU: (Your answer...)

ME: Reminders...
1. Be a Peacemaker...v. 15.
2. Read God's Word...v. 16.
3. Let God's Word be at HOME in your life.
4. Do *"everything in the name of the Lord Jesus!"* v. 17.

That kind of sums up Colossians chapter three.
Using THE MAP regularly will keep you on top of being
God's person.

Want to be a better Wife? Go to the MAP.
Want to be a better Husband? Go to the MAP.
Want to be a better Father? Go to the MAP.
Want to be a better Employee? Go to the MAP.
Want to be a better Employer? Go to the MAP.

YOU: Okay, I got it.

Remember the beginning of this book? **"Therefore, put to death whatever in you is worldly!"** v. 5.

Colossians chapter three has given to you THE MAP of living a life personally in the Messiah.
Unpack the bad stuff and pack the good stuff.
- Unpack "sexual immorality and idolatry..."
- Unpack "anger, wrath, malice, slander, and a filthy mouth..."
- "Stop lying..."
- Become new in Messiah...

ITEMS TO PACK:
- "Be compassionate, humble, kind, patient..."
- Learn how to "forgive as Messiah has forgiven you..."
- "Put on love..."
- Let Peace rule your life...
- Let God's Word be at home in your life...
- "Do everything in the name of the Lord..."
- Wives, "submit..."
- Husbands, "Love..."
- Workers, "Submit to your bosses AS you submit to God..."
- Do "Everything enthusiastically for the Lord...not for men..."

ME: I leave you with this. Paul said in another letter:

Do what you have learned and received and heard and seen in me, and the God of peace will be with you!"
Philippians 4:9